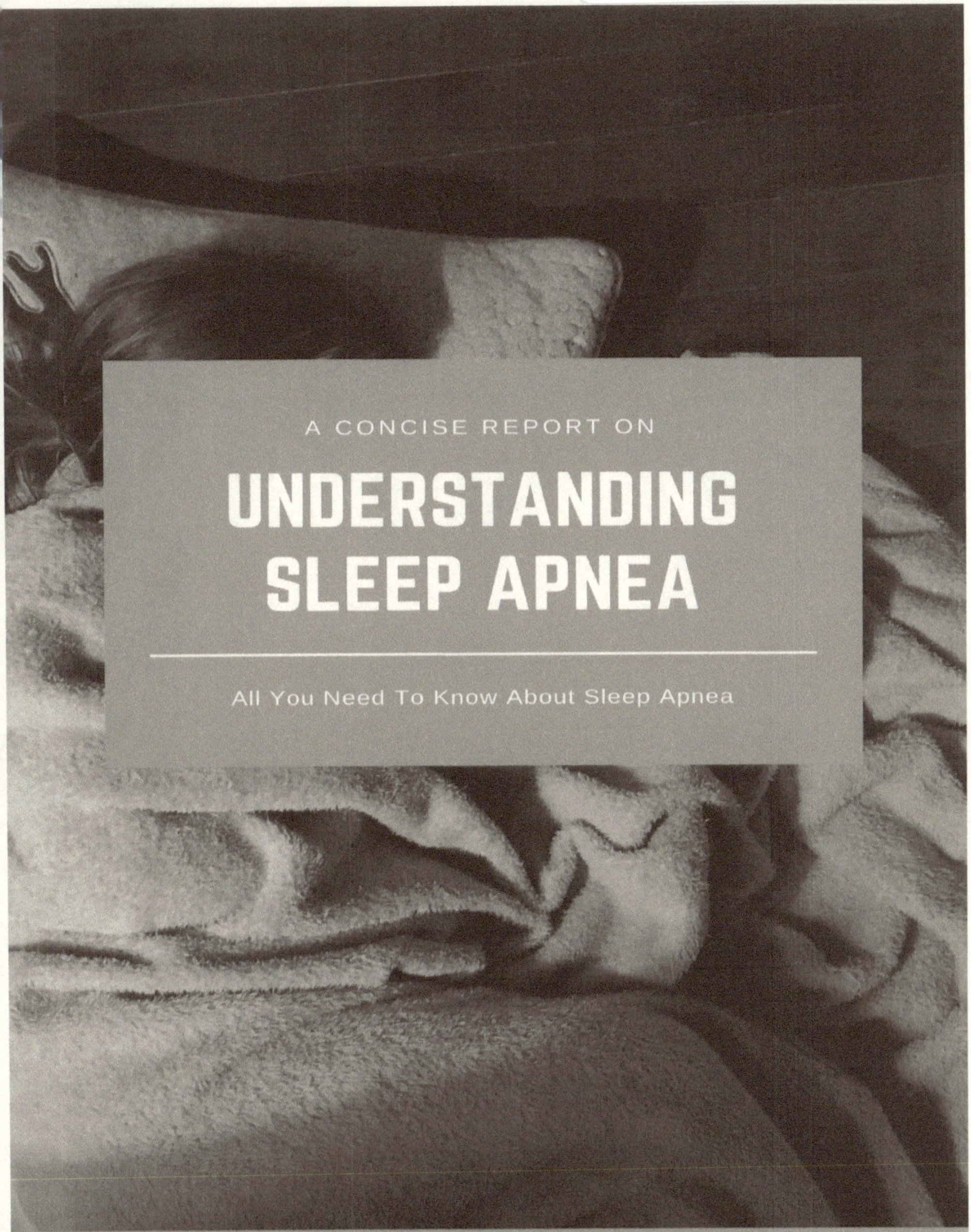

A CONCISE REPORT ON
UNDERSTANDING SLEEP APNEA
All You Need To Know About Sleep Apnea
DR DEVRIN RONJEK, M.D

A CONCISE REPORT ON

UNDERSTANDING SLEEP APNEA

All You Need To Know About Sleep Apnea

DR DEVRIN RONJEK, M.D

UNDERSTANDING SLEEP APNEA

ALL YOU NEED TO KNOW ABOUT SLEEP APNEA

DR DEVRIN RONJEK

CONTENTS

1. Introduction

2. Symptoms of Sleep Apnea

3. Effects of Sleep Apnea

4. Snoring and Sleep Apnea

5. Relationship With Obesity

6. What About Children?

7. Undiagnosed Sleep Apnea

8. Snoring And Sleep Deprivation

9. Noise During Sleep

10. Role Of Genetics

11. Solution For Sleep Apnea

12. Treatment

1

INTRODUCTION

Because many people experience snoring at some point in their lives, certain medical conditions that involve snoring can go unnoticed. Sleep apnea is a serious sleep disorder that involves choking, paused breathing, or shallow breaths during sleep. Because this condition can mimic normal snoring, it often remains undiagnosed.

There are 3 types of Sleep Apnea

- Obstructive - Fairly common
- Central - Rare
- Mixed - Extremely rare

An apnea is a period during which breathing ceases or is dramatically reduced. In general terms, an apnea occurs when a person stops breathing for 10 seconds or longer. This creates a drop in blood oxygen levels and an increase in stress hormones, which can prompt a person to gasp for breath. Related symptoms of sleep apnea include morning headaches, mood swings, sore throat, freqquent urination at night, and cognitive problems.

Sleep apnea occurs in several different types. In central sleep apnea, the brain does not signal the airway muscles to breathe; this breathing difficulty is the result of instability in the respiratory control center and is not due to airway obstruction. Central sleep apnea is often associated with certain medications and medical conditions. The second more-common and more-severe form of sleep apnea is obstructive sleep apnea. This condition is created by airway blockage, usually when the soft tissue at the back of the throat collapses during sleep. Obstructive sleep apnea often causes snoring because of blocked breathing during sleep. This condition is common in individuals who are overweight, but can affect even small children if they have enlarged tissue in their throats.

Sleep apnea is a chronic sleep condition that reqquires long-term management through lifestyle changes, mouthpieces, surgery, and other treatments. If the condition is left untreated, sleep apnea can lead to increasing medical problems, such as high blood pressure, headaches, stroke, heart failure, diabetes, and depression. Additionally, untreated sleep apnea can create poor performance in daily activities as a result of sleep deprivation. This can increase your risk of work accidents, motor-vehicle crashes, and other safety problems. Because of these serious complications, it is vital that you see your doctor to treat any chronic snoring or breathing issues during sleep.

2

SYMPTOMS OF SLEEP APNEA

Over 100 million people suffer from sleep apnea worldwide. Of these individuals, approximately 80% are currently undiagnosed and are at risk for extensive health complications. Sleep apnea is a potentially dangerous sleep disorder that involves repeatedly paused breathing. Those who have sleep apnea often snore loudly and feel exhausted even after a full night's sleep.

An estimated one in 25 middle-aged men and one in 50 middle-aged women have sleep apnea. Ethnic groups such as African-Americans, Hispanics, and Pacific Islanders are more likely to develop sleep apnea than are Caucasians. This condition occurs in two primary forms. In central sleep apnea, the brain does not send appropriate signals to the muscles responsible for breathing. In obstructive sleep apnea, however, the throat muscles relax to the point of hindering airflow. This latter form of sleep apnea is the more common type, affecting middle-aged males predominantly.

Sleep apnea involves several primary symptoms, which may be noticed by the patient or by their sleep partner, roommate, or other household members. If you suffer from sleep apnea, you are often aware of symptoms such as excessive daytime sleepiness, memory and concentration difficulties, headaches, frequent urination during the night, and sweating and chest pain during sleep. Other symptoms are more obvious to your sleep partner and others; these include loud snoring, restless tossing and turning during sleep, nighttime choking or gasping, and frequent pauses in breathing.

These symptoms are generally caused by airway obstruction as a result of enlarged throat tissue or poor airway-muscle tone. If you suffer from these symptoms, see your doctor for a physical exam. He or she may refer you to a specialist for a sleep assessment like a polysomnogram, which measures various body functions during sleep to determine the severity of your breathing impairment. Based on these diagnostics, your medical team will be able to help treat your sleep apnea and to prevent any associated side effects to your cardiovascular health.

3

EFFECTS OF SLEEP APNEA

Many individuals suffer from sleep apnea, a disorder involving paused, irregular, and labored breathing and snoring. If this condition goes untreated, it can create long-term side effects and associated medical risks.

Obstructive sleep apnea, which involves improper relaxation of the throat muscles, causes repeated episodes of partial or complete blockage of the upper airway while sleeping. During one of these obstructive episodes, the body labors to reopen the airway. As a result, breathing resumes with a gasp, choking noise, or body jerk. Because of low oxygen flow to vital organs and unrefreshing sleep, individuals with sleep apnea are at risk for serious complications. Central sleep apnea, which occurs when the brain fails to send the proper signals to the muscles responsible for breathing, is also associated with impaired sleep and related health issues.

As a result of impaired sleep, those with sleep apnea usually feel extremely fatigued during the day. This can limit daytime performance at work and increase the likelihood of accidents or injury while performing tasks like driving a car. Sleep deprivation and relational disruption is also common for the sleep partners of people with sleep apnea.

Cardiovascular issues are also common among sleep apnea patients because of elevated blood pressure. To compensate for impaired oxygen flow, the heart's pumping activity escalates to harmful levels. Obstructive sleep apnea also increases your risk of stroke and brain damage, even if your blood pressure is not high. This condition also creates a higher risk of atrial fibrillation, congestive heart failure, and other vascular disease. In contrast, central sleep apnea is usually the result-not the cause-of heart disease.

People with sleep apnea are also more likely to have abnormal liver function and liver scarring. Additionally, they may experience complications after major surgery and when using certain medications. Depression, mood swings, headaches, and sexual dysfunction are also common for sleep apnea patients. Given these complications, sleep apnea is a serious disorder. See your doctor immediately if you spot any warning signs of this condition to ensure effective treatment and to prevent additional medical issues.

- Sleep apnea can affect anyone, but tends to be more common in men than in women
- It is said to affect 4 percent of adult males and only 2 percent of adult females
- Overweight people are more likely to suffer with it
- Anyone with a neck measurement above 17 inches is said to be more susceptible
- People with a very small or recessed jaw (retrognathia). This increases the chance of the tongue falling back and blocking the airway
- Abnormalities, such as a large uvula (the dangly bit at the back of your throat) or enlarged tonsils
- Much more common as people get older
- Some studies show that it may be hereditary, but this has yet to be verified

Sleep apnoea can also affect children, but thankfully it's rare. There are some that suspect there is a connection to infant cot deaths, but no evidence of this has been found as yet.

4

SNORING AND SLEEP APNEA

Snoring is a common condition that affects approximately 45% of adults occasionally and 25% chronically. Those who experience chronic snoring may be suffering from obstructed breathing or another serious medical condition. An estimated 75% of people who snore have obstructive sleep apnea (OSA), which involves short periods of disrupted breathing during sleep that can lead to long-term health problems.

The most common sign of OSA is loud and continual snoring, sometimes punctuated by choking or gasping. Another common OSA symptom is fighting sleepiness throughout the day. Other symptoms of OSA include morning headaches, concentration difficulty, a dry mouth and sore throat when waking in the morning, and irritability or depression. While OSA almost always involves noisy and frequent snoring, snoring itself does not always indicate that a person has OSA.

The immediate effect of sleep apnea is that the snorer sleeps lightly and keeps his or her throat muscles tense to maintain airflow to the lungs. Because the snorer does not get good rest, he or she is often tired during the day, which can impair job performance and jeopardize your safety. If left untreated, OSA increases your risk of developing cardiovascular illnesses, diabetes, and other medical issues.

Snoring or OSA generally responds to treatments offered by otolaryngologists and other medical professionals. OSA is commonly treated by a nasal mask that opens the airway via exerting a small amount of positive pressure. This form of treatment is called continuous positive airway pressure (CPAP).

Adults who suffer from occasional snoring can benefit from adjusting their lifestyle to include healthy weight loss, more exercise, less alcohol, and regular sleeping patterns. If you or your sleeping partner is experiencing any snoring, impaired breathing during sleep, or increased sleepiness, see your physician to ascertain whether OSA is the cause. He or she can also suggest treatment options and lifestyle changes to relieve these symptoms.

5

RELATIONSHIP WITH OBESITY

In addition to making sleep apnea more likely, obesity can also occur as a result of sleep apnea. Although this relationship is not completely understood by researchers yet, the elevated risk of obesity among sleep apnea patients appears to be caused by the effects of sleep deprivation and its effects on hunger and satiety hormones.

According to the Centers for Disease Control and Prevention, approximately 65% of Americans are now overweight or obese. Sleep apnea and the resulting poor sleep often prompts people to eat more. This is likely due to impaired hormone activity created by sleep deprivation, which leads to harmful metabolic changes. These metabolic and hormonal changes are why many individuals who suffer from sleep apnea have a higher risk of becoming overweight or obese.

When appetite-regulating hormones are operating improperly, it is much easier to overeat and gain weight. Lack of sleep decreases the body's levels of the hormone leptin, which is responsible for signaling the brain when the body is satiated and no longer hungry. Studies have indicated that leptin levels are disrupted in individuals with obstructive sleep apnea; the extent of leptin disruption is not determined by obesity alone, implying that sleep apnea is responsible for the hormonal imbalance, disrupted appetite, and resulting weight gain.

To make matters worse, when your body is sleep-deprived, it

increases its production of ghrelin, which is responsible for stimulating appetite and increasing eating. These unhealthy levels of ghrelin and leptin can prompt overeating, fat storage, and excess weight. As a result, many individuals with sleep apnea are at a much higher risk for becoming overweight or obese.

Sleep is incredibly important for your overall health, and most individuals require seven to nine hours of rest each night. If you are suffering from a sleep disorder like sleep apnea, see your doctor. He or she can recommend lifestyle adjustments and treatments to ensure better rest and a lower risk of weight gain.

Of the 12 million Americans with sleep apnea, over half are overweight. Sleep apnea involves chronically shallow, irregular, or stopped breathing and periodic snoring during sleep. Sleep apnea may be obstructive (when weak throat muscles hinder breathing) or, in rarer cases, central (when the brain fails to signal respiratory muscles).

Although thinner individuals can develop sleep apnea, this condition is most common among people with large neck circumferences (over 17 inches for men and over 16 inches for women). Over half of those with obstructive sleep apnea are overweight or obese, defined as a body mass index (BMI) of 25-29.9 or 30.0 and above, respectively. This is partially because excess weight can form fatty deposits around your upper airway. In addition to creating other problems, these deposits may also obstruct breathing and elevate your risk of cardiovascular complications.

The correlation between excess weight and sleep apnea also works the other way: sleep apnea increases your risk of becoming overweight or obese. Sleep apnea leads to sleep deprivation, which often prompts people to eat more. This is likely due to the relationship between hunger and satiety hormones (leptin and ghrelin) and sleep deprivation, although researchers are not yet certain about the nature of this relationship. To make matters worse, people with sleep apnea often have high blood pressure, high fasting glucose, and high cholesterol. When hunger and satiety hormones are not operating effectively, it is much easier to overeat and gain even more weight. This can aggravate the effects of sleep apnea, worsening hormonal disturbance and eating habits and prompting further weight gain.

The vicious cycle of obesity and sleep apnea can worsen if these disorders are left untreated. If you suffer from sleep apnea, and especially if you are overweight or obese, speak to your doctor to determine the best lifestyle changes, surgical procedures, and treatments for your symptoms.

WHAT ABOUT CHILDREN?

Disordered breathing like obstructive sleep apnea can occur in children as well as in adults. An estimated three to 12 percent of children snore, and one to 10 percent of children suffer from obstructive sleep apnea. Most children with sleep apnea experience relatively mild symptoms and can outgrow the condition, but others are at risk for complications like cardiopulmonary disease, behavioral problems, and failure to thrive.

Sleep apnea is marked by pauses in breathing during sleep, and the condition often involves snoring, gasping, or choking as the person struggles to breathe during these episodes. In general, sleep apnea in children is caused by the enlargement of the adenoids or tonsils. This disorder can occur even in newborns and may create long-term health concerns if not treated. An enlarged tongue may also contribute to long-term snoring and sleep apnea in children.

Another increasingly common cause of obstructive sleep apnea in children is obesity. Children who are overweight or obese can have sleep-apnea-related breathing problems because of fat deposits in the neck and throat that narrow their airways. Alternatively, existing health conditions such as Down syndrome, a cleft palate, and cerebral palsy can create abnormalities in the tongue and jaw or may cause neuromuscular deficits, which may lead to sleep apnea and other breathing issues.

Sleep apnea in children is most common between ages three and six, when adenoids and tonsils are at their largest in relation to child-size airways. A child who snores chronically should be examined by a doctor or an otolaryngologist. He or she may suggest weight loss to reduce fat deposits or surgery to remove the enlarged tonsils or adenoids. For children who are not candidates for surgery or who experience persistent snoring even after surgery, doctors recommend wearing a sleep mask for at least three hours a night to reduce symptoms and promote healthy breathing.

UNDIAGNOSED SLEEP APNEA

Sleep apnea and other sleep disorders have become an increasingly important health concern in the United States. Associated with obesity, depression, and other health concerns, sleep apnea occurs when your airway is blocked by throat tissue or not activated properly by the brain during sleep. Unfortunately, many of those who suffer from this condition have not received an official diagnosis and are therefore not pursuing the treatment they need.

Sleep apnea affects an estimated nine percent of women and 24 percent of men. Although this disorder is treatable and preventable, at least 80 percent of those with moderate to severe sleep apnea are currently undiagnosed. This is dangerous because untreated sleep apnea can also cause high blood pressure, stroke, chronic heart failure, atrial fibrillation, and other cardiovascular complications, in addition to making accidents more likely.

Because of the dangerous consequences of untreated sleep apnea, obtaining an accurate diagnosis is essential for those with this condition. Studies have determined that patients with undiagnosed sleep apnea have considerably higher overall medical costs that correlate with the severity of their sleep-disordered breathing. Other studies indicate that undiagnosed sleep apnea may cause systemic hypertension in middle and older-aged men especially. Furthermore, researchers estimate that estimate that untreated sleep apnea creates approximately $3.4 billion in additional medical costs in the United States.

If you are male, over the age of 40, or overweight, you are at an even higher risk level for developing sleep apnea. Additionally, if any of your family members have chronic sleep disorders, you are more likely to experience one as well. If you are experience trouble sleeping on a regular basis, it is very important that you see your doctor to discuss the possibility of sleep apnea and to consider the solutions that would work best for you.

SNORING AND SLEEP DEPRIVATION

Although many people snore occasionally, it can affect some people frequently and cause significant sleep issues. Snoring can impair the quantity and quality of sleep of you and your family members or roommates. Snoring is a common condition that can affect anyone. It occurs most often, however, in men and in those who are overweight. Additionally, snoring usually becomes worse as you age. Habitual snorers often require medical assistance to get a good night's sleep.

Snoring is caused by the physical obstruction of airflow through the mouth and nose. This obstruction of airflow can be caused by a combination of various factors. Some people snore because of obstructed nasal airways, which can occur during a sinus infection or in allergy seasons. Bulky throat tissues can also aggravate snoring; this is generally a concern for those who are overweight or for children with large tonsils. Additionally, poor muscle tone in the throat and tongue as a result of aging or alcohol consumption can lead to snoring, as relaxed throat muscles can collapse back into the airway and obstruct airflow. Finally, having a long uvula or a long soft palate can narrow the passage between the nose and throat, causing frequent snoring.

Those who suffer from snoring can experience impaired sleep in several areas. Chronic snorers often develop obstructive sleep apnea, which involves interrupted breathing during sleep, waking up frequently during the night, higher blood pressure, and greater risk of cardiovascular issues. Additionally, chronic snorers can hinder the sleep of those around them, causing others to experience drowsiness during the day and an impaired quality of life, which may lead to resentment and strained relationships.

Because sleep deprivation can be detrimental to your mental and physical wellbeing, it is important to consult your healthcare provider to determine how to treat your snoring. To maximize the quality of your sleep and decrease the effects of sleep deprivation, ensure that your snoring and other sleep disorders are treated by a medical professional. He or she can help you develop good sleep habits to prevent snoring and its harmful effects.

Reason Behind Snoring

Many people are affected by snoring, with 25% of adults snoring habitually. Snoring occurs when air cannot move freely through your nose and mouth during sleep, causing tissues in the nose and mouth to vibrate. Generally, this impaired airflow is created by blockage and airway narrowing, either from improper sleep posture or from abnormally shaped soft tissue in the throat. Finding out the specific cause of your snoring is essential to manage it effectively.

Gaining extra weight is a major reason for snoring, since excess weight leads to fatty tissue and poor muscle tone. These problems can create or worsen snoring, since excess tissue can obstruct your airway and poor muscle tone limits the efficiency of your breathing. Sleep posture also prompts snoring. Sleeping flat on your back causes your throat tissue to relax towards your airway, creating additional blockage and vibration.

Age and gender can be contributing reasons for snoring. Once you reach middle age, your throat can become narrower, and the muscle tone in your throat may also diminish. This can lead to snoring that worsens as you continue to age. Before middle age, however, gender can also serve as a reason for your snoring: men are twice as likely as women to snore because of their narrower airways. This is the situation among younger adults, but after women experience menopause, they are just as likely to snore as men.

Nasal and sinus issues such as allergies or congestion can also create blocked airways by limiting inhalation, which can lead to snoring. Also, consuming alcohol or using tobacco can increase muscle relaxation and worsen snoring. Certain medications may also relax throat muscles and prompt snoring.

Chronic snoring can often indicate the presence of a more-serious medical issue such as sleep apnea. To ensure effective treatment for your snoring, speak to your doctor about suspected causes and potential treatments.

NOISE DURING SLEEP

Many individuals are mildly affected by snoring during sleep. For some people, however, snoring can indicate the presence of a more-serious medical condition with additional complications. If your snoring is chronic and involves choking episodes, you are most likely suffering from obstructive sleep apnea.

Sleep apnea is a serious sleep disorder that is created by obstruction from enlarged throat tissue, tonsils, and adenoids. These enlarged structures block upper airway passages during sleep, making breathing labored and difficult. Noisy and persistent snoring is a common sign of obstructive sleep apnea. Pauses of breathing often punctuate snoring in those with this condition, and choking or gasping usually follows these pauses. Individuals with obstructive sleep apnea have continual shallow or irregular breathing during sleep, and may even stop breathing up to hundreds of times per night.

An estimated 12 million people in the U.S. suffer from sleep apnea. During an obstructive sleep apnea episode, the chest muscles and diaphragm labor extensively to open the blocked airway and restore airflow to the lungs. Breathing usually resumes with a loud choking sound, gasp, or body jerk. Someone with sleep apnea generally will not remember these episodes, since the body stirs just enough to tighten the throat muscles and open the windpipe. Sleeping partners of those with sleep apnea are often the first to notice these choking episodes and may become alarmed at the labored breathing of the snorer.

Choking, gasping, and experiencing the other effects of sleep apnea reduces the flow of oxygen to vital organs during sleep, causing irregular heart rhythms and daytime sleepiness. If left untreated, this condition can lead to extensive cardiovascular issues and impair daily activities. See your doctor to address any concerns about choking during sleep and to suggest lifestyle adjustments such as weight loss and quitting smoking. He or she may refer you to a specialist or a surgeon to reduce sleep apnea and related breathing issues.

10

ROLE OF GENETICS

Sleep apnea can create significant health complications for many individuals. This disorder occurs when airflow obstruction during sleep is either caused by the relaxation of the soft palate and tongue, or by disrupted brain signals failing to control the respiratory muscles. This disrupted airflow leads to choking, gasping, and snoring in between episodes. Based on its cause, sleep apnea is referred to as obstructive or central, respectively. Several factors can increase your risk of developing sleep apnea, such as gender, obesity, and family medical history.

Family history is one predictor of obstructive sleep apnea: if you have close relatives with sleep apnea, your risk of having this form of the disorder is increased. This is most likely because sleep apnea and snoring are complex traits, affected by your genetics as well as by environmental factors.

Researchers suggest that given the interrelated pathways regulating weight and other traits involved in sleep apnea, such as ventilatory control, airway muscle function, and sleep characteristics, there are genes with multiple and diverse effects that independently impact obesity and obstructive sleep apnea traits. In addition, negative environmental influences like periodic oxygen deprivation and sleep disruption that are produced by sleep apnea can interact with obesity genes and worsen the effects of snoring and sleep apnea.

Other genetic studies have also found that approximately 40% of the variation in the occurrence and severity of sleep apnea may be explained by familial factors. It seems most likely that specific genetic factors associated with craniofacial structure, body-fat distribution, and neural control of the upper airway muscles interact to create snoring and obstructive sleep apnea.

Multiple racial studies, chromosomal mapping, familial studies, and twin studies support the possible link between obstructive sleep apnea and genetic factors; ergo, most of the risk factors involved in sleep apnea may be regarded as genetically determined, at least in part.

SOLUTION FOR SLEEP APNEA

Sleep apnea is a medical condition that impairs breathing during sleep, causing sleepiness and other health complications. An apnea episode involves a cessation of airflow for 10 to 20 seconds can occur hundreds of times per night. Thankfully, there are several lifestyle changes that can reduce or eliminate your sleep apnea.

Quitting smoking can often relieve breathing issues associated with obstructive sleep apnea, since smoking increases respiratory inflammation and fluid retention in your airway. Your doctor can suggest programs and products to help you quit smoking. Additionally, avoiding alcohol, sedatives, and sleeping pills can also alleviate sleep apnea, as these substances relax respiratory muscles and can impair breathing, especially when taken before sleeping.

Losing weight and exercising are also helpful ways of reducing your sleep apnea. Especially if you are overweight or obese, weight loss can dramatically improve breathing issues and lessen your risk of other health concerns. Losing excess weight can reduce extra throat tissue that may block airflow into the lungs during sleep. Similarly, increased physical activity is also important to develop healthy muscle tone in the lungs and airway. Even 30 minutes of moderate activity most days of the week can alleviate sleep apnea symptoms.

Adjusting your sleeping posture can further relieve issues associated with sleep apnea. Sleeping on your back generally makes your tongue and soft palate rest against the back of your throat, blocking your airway. To ensure that you sleep on your side, try sewing a tennis ball inside a sock to the back of your pajama top. Elevating your head with a foam wedge can also reduce snoring and other breathing issues.

Finally, keeping your nasal passages open at night may also reduce sleep apnea symptoms. Saline sprays, breathing strips, neti pots, decongestants, and antihistamines can temporarily improve nasal airflow and breathing. Ultimately, these remedies can substantially improve your health and relieve sleep apnea. See your doctor to address more serious symptoms of sleep apnea and to explore other medical treatments.

Obstructive sleep apnea (OSA) is the most prevalent sleep disorder in the adult population. Current estimates suggest that moderately severe OSA is present in approximately 11.4% of men and 4.7% of women. OSA is defined as the occurrence of at least five apneas/hypopneas (temporary cessation of breathing) in one hour. Symptoms typically associated with OSA include snoring, excessive daytime somnolence, and restless sleep. Male gender, smoking and alcohol consumption, obesity and aging are known factors associated with a higher propensity for OSA. According to Fietze and colleagues, over the course of 5 years, the incidence of moderate OSA increases by approximately 8%. OSA is associated with a number of medical comorbidities including hypertension, heart failure, myocardial infarction, diabetes mellitus, gastroesophageal reflux disease, and stroke.

Chung and colleagues9 note that the prevalence of OSA is higher in patients presenting for surgery than in the general population. A significant proportion of OSA patients remain undiagnosed when they present for surgery. This is of concern to the perioperative physician, as OSA has been associated with increased perioperative risk and postoperative complications.

Patients with OSA have a higher propensity for perioperative complications following surgery under general anesthesia – Gupta and colleagues found that patients with OSA undergoing hip or knee replacement were at an increased risk of developing perioperative complications (24% versus 9%, respectively).

Proposed guidelines from the Adult Obstructive Sleep Apnea Task Force of the American Academy of Sleep Medicine suggest that questions regarding OSA should be included in routine health screenings. Moreover, if OSA is suspected, a comprehensive sleep evaluation should be conducted. Similarly, the 2006 guidelines published by the American Society of Anesthesiologists recommend collaboration between anesthesiologists and surgeons to develop an evaluation protocol prior to surgery.

However, clinical practices pertaining to the perioperative management of OSA surgical patients are inconsistent. Recent increased attention in this area has revealed a lack of uniformity surrounding practice guidelines for the assessment and management of patients with OSA in the perioperative arena.

The importance of the problem of OSA, both in terms of prevalence and consequences, is driving changes in the way OSA is investigated worldwide. As primary care physicians have become more adept at identifying the problem clinically, these resources have been overwhelmed and lengthy waiting lists have resulted. The expense has also caused access problems for some. This has resulted in increased use of simple home based studies to triage the problem. These are suitable methods to rule in patients with a high pre-test probability on clinical grounds and may prove helpful to anesthesiologists seeking information quickly in patients presenting for pre-anesthetic assessment.

Anesthesiologists also need to be aware that straightforward OSA is on the simpler end of a spectrum of sleep related breathing disorders that include sleep hypoventilation and periodic breathing. The conditions can coexist. Sleep hypoventilation is observed in patients with ventilatory insufficiency due to pre-existing lung disease, respiratory muscle weakness or chest wall problems, including obesity. Periodic breathing is often seen in the context of left ventricular dysfunction or neurological disease. These problems are likely to be of similar significance for anesthesiology, but require more detailed investigation

OSA is a widely prevalent problem and will become an increasing preoccupation of anesthesiologists, partly because as knowledge is developed in this area, the difficult airway is being seen in a broader context than just the perioperative considerations. Prevalence is increasing with increasing obesity and aging.

TREATMENT

The first step is to try and lose weight, stop smoking and reduce your alcohol intake. In some cases of very mild sleep apnea, sleeping on your side instead of your back can help.

If you have been referred to a specialist, you will be given the standard Epworth Sleepiness Test. He may also make arrangements for a comprehensive sleep-study.

The next step I went through was to try a Orthodontic dental appliance which looks rather like a gum shield. It draws the lower jaw forward, making more room at the back of the throat. Spacers are added each month to gradually increase the pressure pushing forward on lower jaw. These are usually made and fitted by a dentist or orthodontist. Try to image what it's like to sleep with this thing in your mouth all night, but I'm told it does work for some people. Didn't work for me.

The CPAP machine (Continuous Positive Airway Pressure) has proven to be the most successful treatment for severe sleep apnea sufferers, but there is a shortage of CPAP machines as they are extremely expensive. This is a medical air pump which is connected via plastic tubing to a nasal or full-face mask. The pressure on the pump is set just high enough to stop the airway collapsing.

Some people find they can't tolerate using a CPAP machine due to the strange experience of having air forced into the lungs. I have met some patients who couldn't bear to have the mask over their face, yet others don't seem to have a problem and some say the noise lulls then to sleep. The CPAP machine certainly does work for OSA and is also a complete cure for snoring.

The Bi-PAP machine is similar to the above machine but is easier for the user to exhale, due to it's bi-level pressures. Bi-PAP machines are not issued very often, due to their excessive cost.

Surgical treatments are also available.

- Trimming nasal passages and removing polyps and other growths to improve nasal breathing.
- Straightening a deviated septum (the middle bit inside your nose) also to aid easier nasal breathing.
- Laser-assisted uvulopalatoplasty (LAUP) using a laser to remove excessive tissue and tightening the throat. Mainly, this operation is used to stop snoring but not always successful and very painful.
- Uvulopalatopharyngoplasty, luckily there's an abbreviation for it (UPPP), which entails removing the uvula (the dangly thing at the back of your throat) plus excess tissue at the back of the throat and part of the soft palate. This is a most unpleasant operation and it didn't cure my OSA. You have to re-learn how to drink, as it can go down the wrong way.

A tracheostomy (alternative spelling tracheotomy) can be done in severe cases where all other treatments have failed. This is the ultimate solution to obstructive sleep apnea, but don't consider this option without a great deal of thought.

www.ingramcontent.com/pod-product-compliance
Lightning Source LLC
Chambersburg PA
CBHW051140250726
48655CB00007B/3159